THE THOUGHTBOOK *of* F. SCOTT FITZGERALD

ALSO PUBLISHED BY THE UNIVERSITY OF MINNESOTA PRESS

Fool for Love: F. Scott Fitzgerald
Scott Donaldson

The Disenchanted
Budd Schulberg

St. Paul's Historic Summit Avenue
Ernest R. Sandeen
Foreword by Larry Millett

Through No Fault of My Own: A Girl's Diary of Life on Summit Avenue in the Jazz Age
Coco Irvine
Introduction by Peg Meier

The Thoughtbook of
F. Scott Fitzgerald

A SECRET BOYHOOD DIARY

F. Scott Fitzgerald

Dave Page, *Editor*

UNIVERSITY OF MINNESOTA PRESS
Minneapolis

The Fesler-Lampert Minnesota Heritage Book Series

Funded by the John K. and Elsie Lampert Fesler Fund and Elizabeth and the late David Fesler, the Fesler-Lampert Minnesota Heritage Book series publishes significant books that contribute to an understanding and appreciation of Minnesota and the Upper Midwest.

Originally published in facsimile by Princeton University Library, 1965.

First University of Minnesota Press edition, 2013.

Published by the University of Minnesota Press
111 Third Avenue South, Suite 290
Minneapolis, MN 55401-2520
http://www.upress.umn.edu

A Cataloging-in-Publication record for this book is available from the Library of Congress.
ISBN 978-0-8166-7977-5 (pb)

Printed in the United States of America on acid-free paper

20 19 18 17 16 15 14 13 10 9 8 7 6 5 4 3 2 1

Contents

Introduction

DAVE PAGE

IN THE SUMMER OF 1910, just before his fourteenth birthday, F. Scott Fitzgerald began keeping a memoir that he titled *Thoughtbook of Francis Scott Key Fitzgerald of St Paul Minn U.S.A.* Perhaps inspired by Violet Stockton, whose "Flirting by Sighns" (the misspelling is Fitzgerald's) figures prominently in the *Thoughtbook*, Fitzgerald penned a somewhat haphazardly organized series of observations until February the following year.

Although most of the vignettes in the *Thoughtbook* are set in St. Paul, where Francis Scott Key Fitzgerald was born on September 24, 1896, several occur in Buffalo, New York, where his family resided for a decade after repercussions from the financial panic of 1893 caused the failure in 1898 of the wicker furniture business run by Scott's father, Edward. In consequence, Edward was forced to take a sales job for Proctor & Gamble in Buffalo. Bouncing between Buffalo and Syracuse, New York, Edward managed to hold his position until 1908, when the family returned to St. Paul. Having developed an early propensity for writing, Scott Fitzgerald set down in pencil snippets of dialogue, lists, and narrative threads from and about his old life in Buffalo and his new one in St. Paul. He complained later that his mother, Molly, had tossed some of his juvenilia, but the *Thoughtbook* was saved.[1]

When Scott and Zelda's daughter Frances (better known as Scottie) donated her father's papers to Princeton University in 1950, the *Thoughtbook* was not included with the original gift, perhaps because it was on loan at the time to Arthur Mizener, a professor at Carleton College in Northfield, Minnesota, who was completing research for his immensely influential 1951 biography of Fitzgerald.

Due to his proximity to his subject's home town, Mizener made frequent trips to St. Paul to interview friends and acquaintances of Fitzgerald. It was "widely known" in those circles, Mizener wrote in *The Far Side of Paradise*, "that Scott kept, locked in a box under his bed, a manuscript known as the 'Thoughtbook,' which was believed to contain candid and destructive accounts of all his contemporaries. This document still exists, fourteen pages torn from a notebook and covered with Fitzgerald's boyish scrawl. It was the source for the 'Book of Scandal' Basil kept."[2] This last sentence refers to a series of *Saturday Evening Post* stories penned by Fitzgerald; known as the Basil stories, some are set at the same time as events described in the *Thoughtbook*. Because Mizener transcribed sample passages from the *Thoughtbook* for his biography, including such "destructive" comments as "I think Una Baches is the most unpopular girl in dancing schools,"[3] he must have had access to the pages before 1951.

With Scottie's permission, parts of the *Thoughtbook* later appeared on February 16, 1959, in a *Life* magazine story called "The Spell of Scott Fitzgerald Grows Stronger." The claim by *Life*'s editors that this was the first time the *Thoughtbook* had been transcribed is simply not true, because passages had appeared earlier in *The Far Side of Paradise*. Written in conjunction with the Broadway success that winter of *The Disenchanted*, a play loosely based on Fitzgerald's life by his friend Budd Schulberg, the article featured the first publication of snippets of letters Fitzgerald wrote to Scottie.

Two years later, *Modern Fiction Studies* included a brief excerpt from the *Thoughtbook* in an essay by Donald Yates titled "The Road to 'Paradise': Fitzgerald's Literary Apprenticeship." Yates does not indicate where he obtained the passage, but because he includes portions of the *Thoughtbook* not incorporated in Mizener's book or the *Life* article, he likely had access to the original or a complete copy.

At some point after 1950, Fitzgerald scholar John Kuehl obtained the original *Thoughtbook* from Scottie. According to Eleanor Lanahan (Scottie's daughter), Kuehl commented about "how casually [Scottie had] lent it to him in the early 50's (left it in a screen door for him)."[4] When Kuehl received the *Thoughtbook*, he noted that, while it still contained fourteen pages, several pages were missing from the beginning.[5] A reproduction of the *Thoughtbook* along with an introduction written by Kuehl appeared in the Winter 1965 issue of the *Princeton University Library Chronicle*. Later that year, a hard-bound reprint of the *Princeton University Library Chronicle* piece was released by the Princeton University Library in a limited edition of three hundred copies. The book suffered from a lack of transcription and the poor quality of its reproduction, as well as from its small press run.

Lanahan assumed that Scottie had given the *Thoughtbook* to Princeton after loaning it to Kuehl. Henry Dan Piper, in his biography of Fitzgerald first published in July 1965, indicated the *Thoughtbook* was located in the Fitzgerald Papers at the Firestone Library, Princeton University.[6] Many scholars presumed the original was there, but it was actually a Photostat copy.[7] The original *Thoughtbook* ended up with biographer Matthew Bruccoli and was donated to the Irvin F. Hollings Special Collections Library at the University of South Carolina, Columbia. Buried deep below ground in a humidity-sensitive room protected by fingerprint- and eye-scan-controlled doors reminiscent of a James Bond film, the *Thoughtbook* is made available only rarely to scholars and the curious. The University of South Carolina provided digital copies to help with the process of transcription for this edition.

I thank the University of Minnesota Press and its editor Erik Anderson for asking me to participate in this project. My sleuthing to discover the provenance of the *Thoughtbook* often took me in unexpected directions, but everyone was as excited as I was about the quest.

By suggesting new paths for me to follow, eminent Fitzgerald scholars Alan Margolies, Jackson Bryer, and James West III helped immensely when I hit dead ends. Without their assistance, this project would have been significantly less complete.

Finally, I thank Mecca Manz, who patiently and calmly listened to my frustrations, often gave me encouragement, and provided the space and time for me to finish this endeavor, a task that began in February 2012 and took one year to complete.

Notes

1 Henry Dan Piper, *F. Scott Fitzgerald: A Critical Portrait* (New York: Holt, Rinehart, and Winston, 1963), 29.

2 Arthur Mizener, *The Far Side of Paradise* (Boston: Houghton Mifflin Company, 1965 [1951]), 17–18.

3 Ibid., 18. Una Baches is one of the very few kids mentioned in the *Thoughtbook* who does not appear in the photograph of Professor Baker's dancing class, so her unpopularity may have driven her away before the picture was taken.

4 Eleanor Lanahan, e-mail message forwarded by Erik Anderson of the University of Minnesota Press to the author, August 6, 2012. Alan Margolies, for whom John Kuehl served as thesis advisor, also remembered that Kuehl mentioned that the *Thoughtbook* was left outside his door (e-mail message to author, February 13, 2012).

5 The fourteen pages Mizener mentioned were still there, but Mizener had not discussed the missing first seven pages. Lanahan, e-mail message, August 6, 2012.

6 Piper, *F. Scott Fitzgerald*, 306, note 32.

7 It is not recorded when that copy was donated. Gabriel Swift, e-mail message to the author, June 29, 2012.

The Thoughtbook of F. Scott Fitzgerald

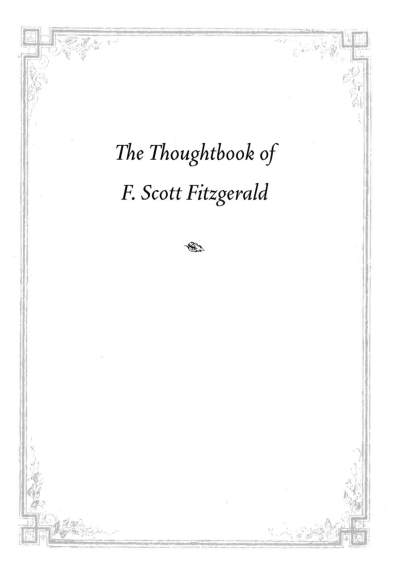

Thoughtbook

of

Francis Scott Key Fitzgerald (*me*)

of

St Paul Minn U.S.A.

Note: The *Thoughtbook* is reproduced here exactly as F. Scott Fitzgerald wrote it, including misspellings, punctuation errors, inconsistencies, and other idiosyncracies and anomalies.

August, 1910

My Girls

My recollections of Nancy are rather dim but one day stands out above the rest. The Gardeners had their home three miles out of town and one day James Imham, Inky for short, my best friend, and I were invited out to spend the day. I was about nine years old Nancy about eight and we were quite infatuated with each other. I was in the middle of the winter so as soon as we got there we began playing on the toboggan. Nancy and I and Inky were on one toboggan and Ham (Nancies big brother) came along and wanted to get on. He made a leap for the toboggan but I pushed off just in time and sent him on his head. He was awful mad. He said he'd kick me off and that it wasn't my toboggan and that I couldn't play. However Nancy smoothed it over and we went into lunch.

Kitty Williams is much plainer to my memory. I met her first at dancing school and as Mr. Van Arnumn (our dancing teacher) chose me to lead the march I asked her to be my pardner. The next day she told Marie Lautz and Marie repeated it to Dorothy Knox who in turn passed it on to Earl, that I was third in her affections. I dont remember who was first but I know that Earl was second and as I was already quite overcome by her charms I then and there resolved that I would gain first place. As in the case of Nancy there was one day which was preeminent in my memory. I went in Honey Chilenton's yard one morning where the kids usually congregated and beheld Kitty. We talked and talked and finally she asked me if I was going to Robin's party and it was there that my eventful day was. We played postoffice, pillow, clapp in and clapp out and other foolish but interesting games. It was impossible to count the number of times I kissed Kitty that afternoon. At any rate when we went home I had secured the coveted 1st place. I held this until dancing school stopped in the spring and then relinquished it to Johnny Gowns a rival. On valentines day that year Kitty recieved no less than eighty four valentines. She sent me one which I have now as also one which Nancy gave me. Along in a box with them is a lock of hair—but wait I'll come to that. That Christmas I bought a five pound box of candy and took it around to her house. What was my surprise when Kitty opened the door. I nearly fell down with embarrassment but I finally stammered "Give this to Kitty," and ran home.

Indians and Violet

Sept 1910

Violet Stockton was a niece of Mrs. Finch and she spent a summer in Saint Paul. She was very pretty with dark brown hair and eyes big and soft. She spoke with a soft southern accent leaving out the r's. She was a year older than I but together with most of the other boys liked her very much. I met her through Jack Mitchell who lived next door to her. He himself was very attached as was Art. Foley and together they sneaked up behind her and cut off her hair that is a snip of it. We had a game we played called Indians which I made up. One side were the Indians and went off and hid somewhere. The cowboys then started off to find them and when the Indians saw their chance they would jump out and take them by surprise. We were all armed with croquet mallets. There were about fifteen of us. Kitty Shultz, Betty Mudge, Betty Foster, Elenor Mitchell, Marie Hersey, Dorothy Green, Violet Stockton and Harriet Foster. The boys were Adolph Sholtz, Wharton Smith, Jack Mitchell, Arthur Foley, Archer Mudge and Roger Foster. Every day for a month we played this and then we turned into truth. At that time I was more popular with girls than I ever have been befor. In truth Kitty Shultz, Dorothy, Violet, Marie and Catherine Tre all liked me best. At the present moment it is the reverse with probably most of these; with at least two, Kitty Shultz and Katherine Tre. However I am wandering from the subject. Finally Violet had a party which was very nice and it was the day after this that we had a quarrel. She had some sort of book called flirting by sighns and Jack and I got it away from Violet and showed it too all the boys. Violet got very mad and went into the house. I got very mad and therefor I *went home. Imediatly Violet repented and called me up on the phone to see if I was mad. However I did not want to make up just then and so I slammed down the receiver. The next morning I went down to Jacks to find that Violet had said she was not coming out that day. It was now my turn to repent and I did so and she came out that evening befor, however I had heard several things, and as I found afterwards so had Violet and I wanted to have justified. Violet and I sat down on the hill back of Shultze's a little away from the others.*

"Violet," I began, "Did you call me a brat."

"No".

"Did you say that you wanted your ring and your picture and your hair back."

"No"

"Did you say that you hated me"

"Of course not, is that what you went home for".

"No, but Archie Mudge told me those things yesterday evening."

"He's a little scamp" said Violet Indignantly.

At this juncture Elenor Mitchell almost went into hysterics because Jack was teasing her, and Violet had to go home with her. That afternoon I spanked Archie Mudge and finished making up with Violet.

Extract from my diary the next day

Wednesday Aug. 20

Didnt do much today but learned a few valuble things to wit

1) that I was a fool to make up with Violet,—From Harriet Foster

2) *that Violet wished she had my teeth from Elenor Mitchell*

3) *that Violet had said that she wanted her ring as soon as she could get it—From Betty Mudge*

Thursday Aug. 21

I learned two things from Betty Mudge

1) *that Violet thought I was a flirt*

2) *that Violet did not like me half as well as she used to*

Friday Aug. 22

I learned in truth

1st) *that Betty Mudges fellows were Bob Harrington, Tim Daniels and Bob Driscoll*

2nd) *that I had a new rival in Wharton Smith*

3d) *that Dorothy's fellows were me and Aurther Foley*

4th *I also learned that as Harriet Foster said Violet said some things that weren't honest*

Mon. Aug 25th

I heard that Violet got mad at me because I got mad so easily from Wharton.

That Kitty Shultzes bows were me and T. Daniels, from her

Dorothy Green said that when I was dippy she liked Wharton Smith better but that usually she liked me better.

Harriet Foster said some sarcastic things as usual

Saturday Aug. 30

I just hate Violet

Jack Mitchell said that Violets opinion of my character was that I was polite and had a nice disposition and that I thought I was the whole push and that I got mad too easily.

Sept. 29th

Not much has happened since Violet went away. The day she went away was my birthday and she gave me a box of candy. Her latest fancy is Arther Foley. He has her ring. She wrote him a letter to ask him for his picture.

* *

And that is the story of Violet Stockton.

November 1910

One day Marie Hersey wrote me a note which began either "Dear Scott I love you very much or I like you very much," and ever since then she has been rather shy when she meets me. Dorothy Green and Caroline Clark are tomboys

Bob Clark is interesting to talk to because he lets me do a lot of talking (which I like) and not like some people I know of never letting you get a word edgewise.

I had a midnight conversation one night with Jim and Cecil and afterwards found that Susan Rice had heard very word of it from her front window. Alida Bigelow is the most popular girl I know of. I know five boys who like her best.

These are the boys and girls I like best in order

First three boys are tie.

Art	*This list*	*Alida Bigelow*
Bob	*changes*	*Margaret Armstrong*
Cecil	*continually*	*Kitty Schulz*
Shumier	*Only*	*Elizabeth Dean*
Boardmen	*authentic*	*Marie Hersey*
Bigelow	*at*	*Dorothy Green*
Sturgis	*date*	*Caroline Clark*
Jim	*of*	*Julia Door*
D. Driscoll	*chapter*	
R. Washington		
Paul	*When I first came to St. Paul*	
Speply	*these were my favorite*	
Rube	boys	girls
Mitchell	*Wharton Smith*	*Violet Stockton*
Smith	*Arthur Foley*	*Dorothy Green*
Smith	*Adolph Sholtz*	*Harriet Foster*

This is an extract from something I wrote after dancing school in Buffalo one night.

Fri Jan 19, 1908

I just love Kitty Williams. Today in dancing school I told her she was my best girl. I dared Earl Knox to say "I love you Kitty," to her and he did it. Then I did too. She asked me if I liked dancing school and I said I liked it if she went. Then she said she liked it if I went. (11 years old)

O Fudge

The looks of the girls

1st	*(1911) Kitty Schultze*	*(1912) Elenor Alair*
2nd	*Alida Bigelow*	*Kitty Schultz*
3rd	*Elenor Alair*	*Marie Hersey*
4th	*Marie Hersey*	
5th	*Julia Dorr*	

Paul and Art. Chap. VI

Feb. 12, 1911

I devote a whole chapter to these two because for a long time they were my ideals but latly one has fallen in my estimation. For a long time I was Pauls ardent admirer. Cecil and I went with him all the time and we thought him a hero. Physically he is the strongest boy I have ever seen and he is a fine foot ball, baseball and tennis player and a fair Hockey player and swimmer. All last winter we three went together and skeed a lot but since I have gone with Bob Clark however I have not liked Paul half so well. In the first place we thought Paul a hero and be both considered him our best friend. He was awfully funny strong as an ox, cool in the face of danger, polite and at times very interesting. Now I don't dislike him. I have simply out grown him.

Feb. 12, 1911

Chap. VII Dancing school in 1911

Since dancing school opened this last time I have deserted Alida. I have two new crushes, to wit—Margaret Armstrong and Marie Hersey. I have not quite decided yet which I like the best. The 2nd is the prettiest. The 1st the best talker. The 2nd the most popular with T. Ames, J. Porterfield, B. Griggs, C. Read, R Warner, ect. and I am crazy about her. I think it is charming to hear her say, "Give it to me as a comp-pliment" when I tell her I have a trade last for her. I think Una Bachus is the most unpopular girl in dancing schools. Last year in dancing school I got 11 valentines and this year 15. Dorothy Green sent a valentine to every girl and one to every boy. There are 3 new girls and one new boy in dancing school this year. The girls are Constance James, Elenor Elair, and Margaret Winchester. The new boy is William Landig. I have a season engagement for every dance up to the ninth. We boys got up a petition to get E. Elair into dancing school and gave it to Mrs. Townsend. We are going to get up another petition to be taught the Boston. One day about a week ago some of the boys including Arthur Foley, Cecil Reade, Donald Bigelow, and Lawrence Boardman refused to do the Grand March. They went out in the hall and began to put on their shoes. Mr. Baker almost had a fit but his efforts to make them march were unavailing. Those of us that were in the march messed it up every which way so now the grand march is abolished and we have three other dances in its place.

Chap. VIII The gooserach and other clubs

Feb. 24–11

The first club I remember really belonging to was "the white handkerchief," Arthur and I were the originators of this and later we admitted Adolf Sholtz and George Gardner. Then came Cecil Reade and Phil Foley making six members. Our first meeting was held in the yellow house next to Michell's old house. Adolph Sholtz was elected president and I secretary dues were fixed at 5 cents per fortnight 5 cents a week being considered too exravagant. Ours was a secret society and we were bound to tell none of the secrets tho I doubt muchly if there were any to tell. This club died a natural death unlike the next one I was in which came to a sudden and dramatic ending. The members were H. Green, P. Ballion, Cecil Reade and me and we entitled ourselves the "boy's secret service of St. Paul." I was chief scout, Cecil chief spy; Paul President, and Harold Green Cheif detective. The "finis" of this club is narrated in the chapter on Paul and Art. Once I belonged to a cruelty to animals society and Betty Mudge told them that I cut of rats tails and so I received a note signed by ten girls telling me politly but firmly that I was fired from the organization.

The best club I ever belonged to was the Gooserah club gotten up by myself. The club originated with the name. There was a boy in our Sunday school class named Alfred Gusan and they call him Goosan. One day quite by accident Paul said Rah for Goose Gooserah. The absurdity of the name struck us and I sugested that we get up a club named this. The first member was Cicil and Paul and I subjected him to a most horrible initiation which consisted of having him eat raw eggs and operating on him with saw cold ice, and needle accomanied by a basin. Then we initiated Sam Stugis, Jim Porterfield, Bob Clark, and Bobby Shurmier. There was a rival organization gotten up by Art, Don and Laurie intitled the belephants and from the first we were sworn enemies We cleared out Cecil's 3d floor for a club room and part of the basement for a gymnasium which (is) was quite creditable. It consisted of 4 pairs dumb bells, 2 pairs Indian clubs, 2 pairs (8 gloves) boxing gloves, 1 pair rist exercisers 1 punching bag 1 wall exerciser, 1 trapeze, 1 pair swinging rings. Paul was the boxing master and Bob Shurmier and I were the fencing teachers. There were 3 degrees in the club: 1st, 2nd & 3d the first degree is anyone who has been initiated, 2nd anyone who has been or is an officer and the 3d anyone who renders an especial service to the club. That summer the club disbanded and so far this winter we have had 2 meetings in one of which were voted in 3 members and the second in which we initiated them. The new members are D. Bigelow, L. Shepley, M. Seymour respectively.

Chap IX Alida & Margaret

Feb. 24

This chapter should be named Margaret & Alida but when I wrote this name in the index I liked Alida best so it is excusably

I am just crazy about Margaret Armstrong and I have the most awful crush on her that ever was. This has been the case ever since Bob's party. She is not pretty but I think she is very attractive looking. She is extremely gracful and a very good dancer and the most interesting talker I have ever seen or rather heard. One Saturday night I was surprised by a visit from Margaret asking me to the Bachus school dance. Of course I accepted with pleasure and that night took her to it. I had a fine time including four dances from Margaret. The next day Julia invited a large crowd of boys and girls to make a visit to a house on Pleasant Ave. that was said to be haunted. Of course we went and the bad part of it was that Jim walked all the way out with Margaret and I was left in the lurch. Jim did not have such a walkover going back because I was on the other side of Margaret but just the same I felt pretty glum that night for I knew that up to that time I had been almost first with Margaret for a week and now Jim had to step in and cheat me. Wednesday an eventful day dawned clear and warm. Jim Porterfield and I were invited to call on Elizabeth Dean by Elizabeth and when we got there we found her *too and we started out for a walk. Margaret and Jim walked ahead and Elizabeth and I behind. This made me mad and this was further inflamed when they got a block ahead of us. Then Elizabeth told me some things. She said that Margaret had given her a note the day befor in school which said "I know I am fickle but I like Jim just as much as I do Scott." When I learned this I was jealous of Jim as I had never been of anyone before. I said some ridiculous things about how I was going to get even with him in Margarets estimation when we reached the country club. Elizabeth went ahead and asked Margaret which of us she liked the best. Margaret said she liked me best. All the way home I was in the seventh heaven of delight. The next time I saw Margaret was Friday. I met Elizabeth and she on the corner near Cecil's house and we talked about 5 minutes.*

[A note that says *"Margaret's Hair"* is on this page.]

Then I took Margaret home and I told her I was invited to the sophmore assembly by C Jame[s] *and she said that she would have invited me if she had thought of it. I had three invites because when I got home I found that Alida Bigelow had invited me also. As Margaret and I walked along we had quite an interesting conversation.*

Said I *"Jim was so confident the other night that you had a crush on him."*

"Well Jim gets another think."

"Shall I let him know you don't like him."

"No: but you can let him know that he isn't first."

"I'll do that"

"Now if you had thought that it might be different."

"Good" said I

"Good" repeated she and then the converstion lagged. She asked me to call for her at eight and go to the play with her and I said yes. Then we said good bye & I went home. Then, sad to say, Margaret called me up & said that she couldn't go. The play was very good but Margaret was not there boo hoo.

One Saturday night about two weeks later my finish came we were over at Ben Griggs four boys, Reub, Ben, Ted & I, and four girls Margaret, Marie, Elizabeth & Dorothy & that evening Margaret got an awful crush on Reuben which at the time I write this is still active. More about Margaret later on.

Alida is considered by some the prettiest girl in dancing school. Bob Clark, E. Driscoll, D. Driscoll, A. Foley, and I all had a crush on her last winter and this fall. Every night Bob & I would go over to see Don (?) & incidently see Alida. She liked Art 1st, Egbert 2nd I third & Bob 4th. Bob is south now & writes her a letter 3 times a week.

Fitzgerald at age fifteen, taken while he was a student at Newman Academy in New Jersey just a few months after he finished the *Thoughtbook*. F. Scott Fitzgerald Papers, Manuscripts Division, Department of Rare Books and Special Collections, Princeton University Library.

514 Holly Avenue, St. Paul, Minnesota, where Fitzgerald lived when he began keeping the *Thoughtbook*. He later used the diary as the basis for "The Book of Scandal" in his Basil Duke Lee stories. Photograph by Alan Ominsky. Courtesy of the Minnesota Historical Society.

509 Holly Avenue, St. Paul, known as the Shotwell House. Stuart B. Shotwell had been killed in an auto accident on May 22, 1910, and the young Fitzgerald, an eyewitness to the accident, was interviewed for the newspaper. Most of the *Thoughtbook* was written in this house; Fitzgerald kept the diary stored safely in a locked box under his bed. Photograph by Alan Ominsky. Courtesy of the Minnesota Historical Society.

The costume party celebrating the end of Professor Baker's dancing class, Ramaley Hall, St. Paul, April 1910. Most of the kids who appear in the *Thoughtbook* are in this photograph. *First row:* McNeil Seymour, Leonard Shepley, Betty Hester, Archie Jackson, Hamilton Hersey, Betty Mudge, Eleanor Mitchell, Cecil Read, Henry Adams, Truman Gardner. *Second row:* Dorothy Greene, Kitty Schulze, Margaret Horn, Egbert Driscoll, Elizabeth Field, Marie Hersey, Alida Bigelow, Helen James, Margaret Armstrong, Julia Door, Joanne Orton, Professor Baker.

Third row: Donald Driscoll, Jim Porterfield, Arthur Foley, Larry Boardman, Georgie Ingersoll, Suzanne Rice, Caroline Clark, Donald Bigelow, Robert Clark, Dorothy Anderson, Jean Ingersoll, Gus Schurmeier. *Fourth row:* Ted Townsend, Jack Mitchell, Mildred Bishop, Priscilla Adams, Wharton Smith, Theodore Ames, Elisabeth Dean, Kitty Ordway, Philip Stringer, Lovell May, F. Scott Fitzgerald. Photograph by Randolph R. Johnson. Courtesy of the Minnesota Historical Society.

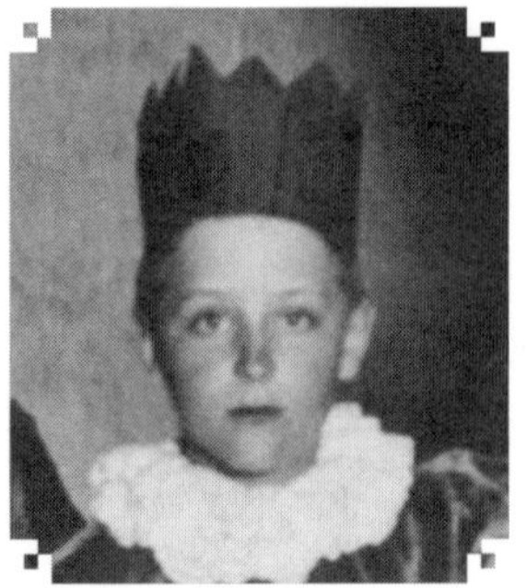

F. Scott Fitzgerald

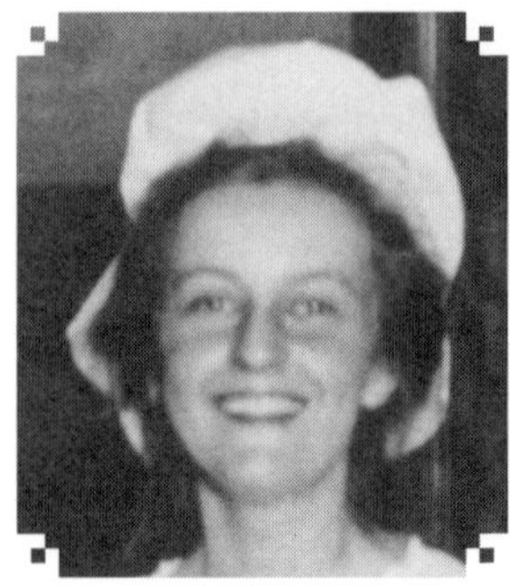

Katherine "Kitty" Schulze

Marie Hersey

Cecil Read

Betty Mudge

Robert Clark

6 THE SAINT PAUL PIONEER PRESS, SUNDAY, SEPTEMBER 6, 1914.

MILITIA AT BUTTE EXPECTS LONG STAY

Court House Is Decorated With Flags and Guardsmen Draw New Supplies.

MINES TO CLOSE MONDAY

Workmen Will Attend Monster Celebration—Labor Day Parades Are Barred.

WOULD IMPEACH OFFICIALS.

Butte, Mont., Sept. 5.—A movement to impeach Mayor Lewis J. Duncan of Butte, and Sheriff Timothy Driscoll of Silver Bow county was inaugurated here tonight when Major Dan J. Donohue, commander of the militia, maintaining martial law, gave citizens permission to have the district court opened long enough to file a petition.

No Arrests Made.

Mines to Close Labor Day.

TRAIN IS HELD UP, 2 PASSENGERS SHOT

Masked Bandits Board Grand Trunk Coaches, Get Loot and Escape.

One May Die.

Board Train in City Limits.

Elizabethan Dramatic Club to Play For Benefit of Baby Welfare Fund

MEMBERS of the cast of the play, "Assorted Spirits," to be presented Tuesday evening at the Y. W. C. A. auditorium under the auspices of the Y. W. C. A. Left to right, upper picture, Elynor Alair, Alice Lyon, Dorothy Greene, Katherine Schulze, Margaret Armstrong, Betty Mudge. Below, McNeil Seymour, Robert Clark, Scott Fitzgerald, Gustav Schurmeier, John Mitchell and Joseph B. Armstrong.

Members of Younger Set in Cast of Production Tuesday at Y. W. C. A.

The Baby Welfare association will be the beneficiary of the play, "Assorted Spirits," which is to be presented by the Elizabethan Dramatic club at the Y. W. C. A. auditorium Tuesday evening.

The playlet was written by Scott Fitzgerald, who also takes a leading role. Miss Elizabeth Magoffin is directing the production.

The cast is composed of members of the younger set and is as follows:

This is the fourth playlet presented by the Elizabethan club.

SOIL CALLS NEGRO, SCHOOL MAN SAYS

Founder of Southern Institution Declares Freedom and Fortune Await Him There.

Graduate of Iowa "U."

BONES THOSE OF A HUMAN

GOES TO RESCUE OF KARLUK SURVIVORS

Third Ship Sails for Wrangell Island and Fourth Will Follow.

Fourth Boat to Sail.

BOARD SEES HOPE IN COUNTY SANATORIA

Tuberculosis Situation in State Hospitals to Be Relieved by Local Institutions.

155 WARDS HAVE DISEASE

Reports Compiled by Control Body Show All Cases of Plague Are Reported.

Two Already Completed.

155 Cases in Hospitals.

Summary of Cases.

Explain Discrepancy.

Will Relieve Conditions.

The Elizabethan Dramatic Club in St. Paul, which included many of Fitzgerald's friends from the dancing school in the *Thoughtbook*. The caption beneath the photograph states "the playlet was written by Scott Fitzgerald, who also takes a leading role." From the *St. Paul Pioneer Press*, September 6, 1914. Courtesy of the Minnesota Historical Society.

Amherst Wilder House, looking up Ramsey Hill in St. Paul, 1892 (now demolished). One of the grandest homes along Summit Avenue, this was the home of Fitzgerald's friend Katherine "Kitty" Schulze, who figures prominently in the *Thoughtbook*. Photograph by A. F. Raymond. Courtesy of the Minnesota Historical Society.

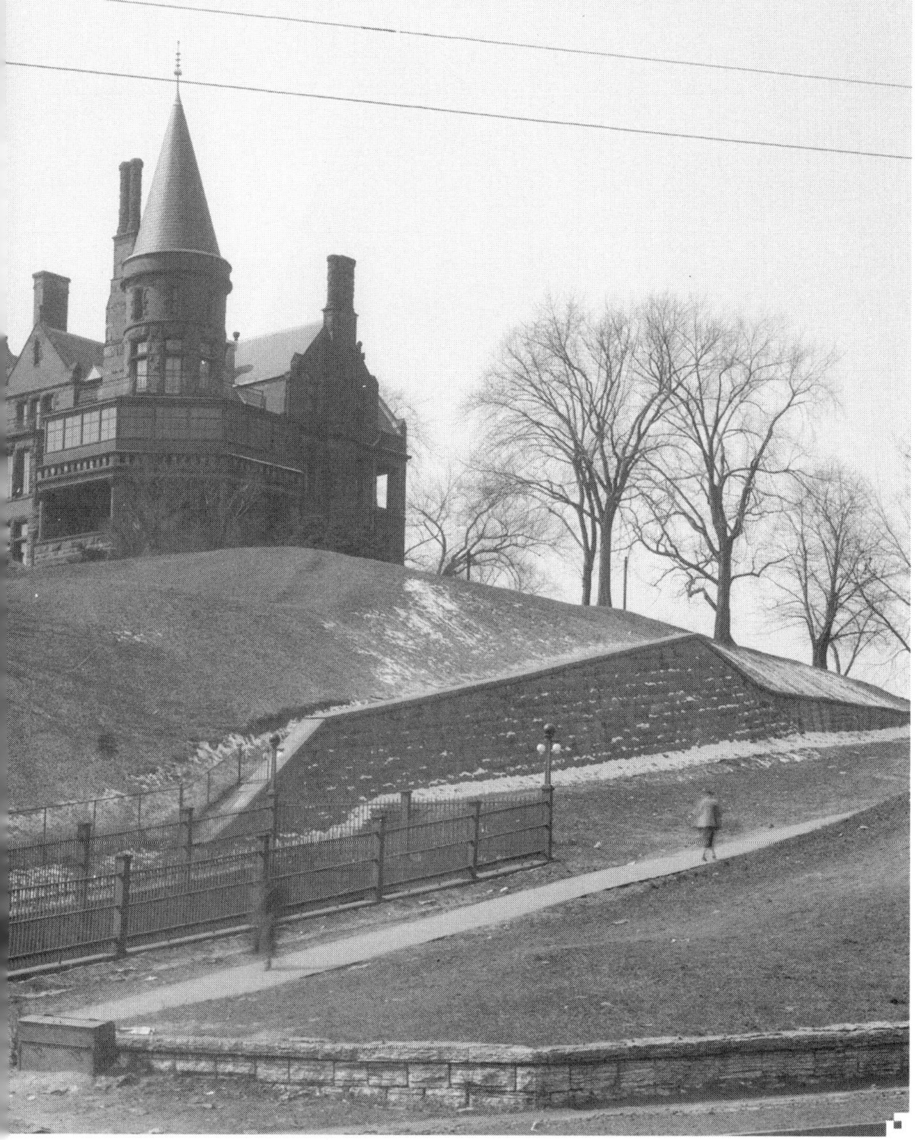

Afterword

Dave Page

Scott Fitzgerald's *Thoughtbook* is perhaps most interesting because of its mood and voice: upbeat and almost completely without guile. In contrast to what Fitzgerald later wrote about this early period of his life, the *Thoughtbook* is downright cheerful. When John O'Hara asked Fitzgerald in a letter in 1933, "I wonder why you do the climber so well. Is it the Irish in you? *Must* the Irish always have a lot of climber in them?"[1] Fitzgerald responded:

> I am half black Irish, and half old American stock with the usual exaggerated ancestral pretensions. The black Irish half of the family had the money and looked down upon the Maryland side of the

> family who had, and really had, that certain series of reticence and obligations that form under the poor old shattered word "breeding" (modern form "inhibitions"). So being born in that atmosphere of crack, wisecrack and countercrack, I developed a two-cylinder inferiority complex.... I spent my youth in alternately crawling in front of the kitchen maids and insulting the great.
>
> I suppose this is just a confession of being a Gael though I have known many Irish who have not been afflicted by this intense social self-consciousness.[2]

The *Thoughtbook* shows a high degree of self-awareness, but it does not possess an excess of self-consciousness in the sense of the word that Fitzgerald meant in his reply to O'Hara—that the subject was somehow embarrassed or ashamed.

The poor person who struggles and succeeds is a favorite theme in American literature, and Fitzgerald regularly applied that trope to his own life. "One afternoon," he told a reporter about an occurrence in Buffalo thirty years before, "the phone rang and my mother answered it. I didn't understand what she said, but I felt that disaster had come to us. My mother, a little while before, had given me a quarter to go swimming. I gave the money back to her. I knew something terrible had happened and I thought she couldn't spare the money now. 'Dear God,' I prayed, 'please don't let us go to the poorhouse.' A little later my father came home. I had been right. He had lost his job." Fitzgerald concluded that the incident caused is father to lose "his essential drive, his immaculateness of purpose."[3] No such bleak pronouncements appear in the extant pages of the *Thoughtbook*.

Besides Fitzgerald's own belated comments about his family's wealth, the myth that Fitzgerald was a poor boy persists because of an unfortunate choice of metaphor that Malcolm Cowley used in his 1953 essay "Fitzgerald: The Romance of Money." Fitzgerald regarded himself, Cowley wrote, "as a pauper living among millionaires, a Celt among

Sassenachs, and a sullen peasant among the nobility. . . . It was as if all his fiction described a big dance to which he had taken, as he once wrote, the prettiest girl . . . and as if he stood at the same time outside the ballroom, a little Midwestern boy with his nose to the glass, wondering how much the tickets cost and who paid for the music."[4] Although Cowley meant to emphasize what he called Fitzgerald's "double vision," the Dickensian image of the hapless waif almost begging for acceptance continues to be associated with Fitzgerald. For example, an editorial in the *Minneapolis Star Tribune* in 1995 made a reference to one of Fitzgerald's lines in the short story "The Popular Girl" that Summit Avenue was "a museum of American architectural failure." The writer went on to say, "But F. Scott Fitzgerald wasn't fully objective; he never made the inner circle of the avenue's wealthy."[5]

Bryant Mangum, in *A Fortune Yet: Money in the Art of F. Scott Fitzgerald's Short Stories*, elaborates on Cowley's phrase. "Double vision denotes two ways of seeing," Mangum explains. "It implies the tension involved when Fitzgerald sets things in opposition in such a way that the reader can, on the one hand, sensually experience the event about which Fitzgerald is writing, immersing himself emotionally in it, and yet at the same time retain the objectivity to stand back and intellectually criticize it."[6] Fitzgerald himself blatantly uses this "double vision" image throughout his fiction. In *The Great Gatsby*, the narrator, Nick Carraway, is a guest at Tom and Myrtle's apartment but also visualizes what its line of yellow windows would look like to a passerby: "I was within and without, simultaneously enchanted and repelled by the inexhaustible variety of life."[7] Later, Nick describes the appeal of New York crowds, of taxis full of men and women headed toward the theater district: "Imagining that I, too, was hurrying toward gayety and sharing their intimate excitement, I wished them well."[8]

In the *Crack-Up* essays, Fitzgerald expanded on this concept of double vision: "the test of a first-rate intelligence," he penned in 1936, "is the ability to hold two opposed ideas in the mind at the same time, and still retain the ability to function."[9] Fitzgerald borrowed the concept from Keats, his "favorite author," according to Cowley.[10] Keats called the effort "'negative capability': the ability to hold conflicting perspectives in the mind without 'irritable' reaching after uncertainty."[11]

John Kuehl noted the connection between Fitzgerald and Keats and the concept of "double vision":

> Like Keats, Scott Fitzgerald struggled between "objectivity" and "subjectivity," and, again like Keats, he was primarily a "subjective" writer. After his death, several American critics began to take this dualism into account. John Dos Passos called his work "a combination of intimacy and detachment"; Malcolm Cowley, "a sort of double vision." But however they phrased it, the critics agreed that it was the author's ability to participate in his fiction and at the same time to stand aside and analyze that participation that gave his work maturity and power.[12]

Mangum ties Fitzgerald's double vision to the author's material and themes, or what Fitzgerald called "the stamp that goes into my books so that people can read it blind like Braille."[13] Mangum lists Fitzgerald's themes as "youth, wealth and beauty."[14] In *This Side of Paradise*, according to Mangum, the three themes revolve around "taking things hard. . . . Event after event in the novel shows Amory taking hard the absence of wealth and the ephemerality of beauty."[15] Intentional or not, the picture Mangum leaves a reader is that Amory is deprived when in actuality the novel presents a more complicated biography of the protagonist. In the first line of the novel, we learn that Amory's father "grew wealthy at thirty through the death of two elder brothers" and later on the page that his mother came from wealthy stock from Lake Geneva, Wisconsin. Amory admits that his college allowance, "while liberal, was not at all what he had expected"[16] and bemoans to his friend Kerry, "We're the damned middle class, that's what!"[17] Above them were no doubt young men whose freedom with money, like Tom Buchanan's in *The Great Gatsby*, "was a matter for reproach,"[18] yet below them in Princeton's caste system were those students who had attended public high schools.

The fact that many of Fitzgerald's stories, including *The Great Gatsby*, utilize "the wealthy insider/poor outsider theme"[19] simply adds to the assumption that Fitzgerald lived on the circumference of the circle of wealth, getting just enough of a glimpse into the lifestyle of the upper class to provide details for his prose. That portrait, however, is a bit distorted. It is true that his father came west from Maryland a couple of decades after the Civil War, searching for the fortune that had eluded him in his home state. He landed in St. Paul and held a series of sales jobs, what the local *City Directory* called "mnfr's agt." His fortune changed in 1890 when he married Mollie McQuillan, the daughter of a wholesale grocer who had amassed a large fortune before he passed away at an early age. The couple wed in Washington, D.C. The governor of Minnesota attended the reception, held in what the *Washington Post* called the McQuillan residence at 1315 N Street.[20] The Fitzgeralds then honeymooned in Europe.

A year or so after the nuptials, Edward moved out of his St. Paul bachelor quarters in the Albion Hotel into the McQuillan mansion, the gaudiest house in Lowertown St. Paul.[21] Within another year, his new entry in the *City Directory* listed him as president of American Rattan & Willow Works, but the title may simply have been for appearances' sake, since subsequent research has failed to disclose any substantive information about the company.[22] As families of means emigrated from Lowertown to the bluffs surrounding St. Paul, the Fitzgeralds and McQuillans also moved to the Summit Hill neighborhood, the most prestigious in the city.

Mollie and Edward took lodgings within a short walk of the premier addresses along Summit Avenue. When their first son was born, they were residing in what was described as one of Summit Hill's first luxury apartment buildings. While small, just two bedrooms, it did provide quarters for a servant and was located just a few blocks down Laurel Avenue from Grandmother McQuillan's elegant townhome.

Even after their move to Buffalo, the Fitzgerald family was far from destitute. They continued to live in nice apartments or homes. Always fearful of her son's health, Mollie took Scott to Washington, D.C., during his first winter in Buffalo, where they settled into one of the most glamorous apartment hotels in the city. Located at 1615 Q Street Northwest, the Cairo had opened late in 1894 amid much fanfare and criticism. Built at a then-record cost of $425,000 in a neo-Moorish/Art Nouveau design, the Cairo stood an unprecedented 156 feet tall. Neighbors complained, and Congress restricted future buildings to 130 feet, a law that still exists to this day.

Despite unfavorable reviews from some architectural critics and fears that it would collapse in a strong wind, the hotel prospered by offering wealthy Americans the kind of elegance to which they had become accustomed during trips to Europe. "Its elaborate entrance," a centennial brochure explains, "welcomed guests and residents into a grand lobby that extended into the building's rear courtyard, where it was lighted by a skylight. In the center of the lobby, surrounded by classical pillars, was a marble fountain."[23] The hotel's amenities included a ballroom, barbershop, bakery, billiard room, bowling alley, and tropical roof garden. Quick to gain prestige, the hotel soon boasted such residents as Taft's vice president (James S. Sherman) and inventor Thomas Edison, who no doubt appreciated the building's electric lighting.

According to Scott's *Ledger*, during the years he lived in New York, the family vacationed regularly in Atlantic City or Lake Placid in the Adirondacks. He spent one summer at a camp in Canada. To be sure, there were complaints: "All the other boys have pocket money," he wrote in a letter to his mother, asking for a dollar while at camp.[24] When Edward lost his job with Proctor & Gamble, it was not the case that the family was destined for the "poorhouse," as Fitzgerald so melodramatically recalled much later. The Fitzgeralds simply returned to St. Paul and survived on Mollie's share of the McQuillan family's wealth as "pieces of family property were sold."[25] Precarious as it may sound, the family's status was far from pitiable.

In St. Paul, Scott attended private preparatory school at St. Paul Academy and once more enjoyed the opportunities to sharpen his dancing skills, as he had done in Buffalo —this time with the children of St. Paul's elite families at Professor Baker's dancing class. He spent summer vacations with his friends in the resort village of Frontenac, Minnesota, a sleepy town made desirable as a getaway by James J. Hill.[26] Mollie, Scott, and sister Annabel, could afford to travel by steamer across the Great Lakes to visit relatives back east. A year and a half after his last entry in the *Thoughtbook*, Fitzgerald's parents sent him to Newman School in Hackensack, New Jersey. Its sixty students were "drawn from the Roman Catholic families of wealth in all parts of the United States." The fee was $850 a year.[27] Although financial comparisons are difficult to make, the sum is easily the equivalent of $25,000 today. When it came time to choose a college, for Scott it was Princeton or nothing. His Aunt Annabel McQuillan[28] had offered to underwrite his education at Catholic Georgetown University, where his father had matriculated, and, to save money, there was talk of sending him to the University of Minnesota, but the death of Grandmother McQuillan in the summer of 1913 solved the problem. "When she received her share of her mother's estate," Broccoli wrote, "Mollie may have had as much as $125,000 in capital."[29]

Having led such a relatively privileged life, Fitzgerald—not surprisingly—does not reveal much angst in the pages of the *Thoughtbook*. The dramatized scenes exhibit Scott in all his childhood charm, vanquishing foes and getting the prettiest girl. The portrait of the artist as a young man shows him as a leader among his peers, not as an interloper peeking through the windows. Benjamin Griggs, one of the boys mentioned in the *Thoughtbook* and a Summit Avenue resident, thought of Scott as "vivacious, interested in people, a leader, a center of conversation. He had a very bright mind."[30] Bob Clark, another name that frequently crops up in the *Thoughtbook*, remembered the "very fine parties" at the home of Louis Hill, James J. Hill's son. "It was not through his parents that he [Fitzgerald] went there," Clark wrote. "Simply as a member of our age group."[31] St. Paulite

Norris Jackson, a Princeton classmate of Fitzgerald's who would eventually marry the sister of Ted Ames, another boy listed in the *Thoughtbook*, scoffed at the idea that Fitzgerald was an outsider. "He was always one of us," Jackson insisted.[32]

Besides serving as a time machine to give us a glimpse into Fitzgerald's childhood mood, the *Thoughtbook* provides readers with an artifact of some of Fitzgerald's earliest writing. According to his *Ledger*, his literary debut occurred in January 1907, when he was eleven and living in Buffalo. "He began a history of the U.S. and also a detective story about a necklace that was hidden in a trapdoor under the carpet," the entry for that month noted, then added, "Wrote celebrated essay on George Washington & St. Ignatius." Two and half years later, in a *Ledger* entry from June 1909, he listed three more literary efforts: "Wrote The Mystery of the Raymond Mortgage. Also 'Elavo' (or was that in Buffalo) and a complicated story of some knights."

Of these half dozen pieces, only "The Mystery of the

Raymond Mortgage" still exists. It was originally printed by the St. Paul Academy arts magazine *Now and Then* in October 1909 and reprinted in March 1960 by *Ellery Queen's Mystery Magazine*. "The Mystery of the Raymond Mortgage" has more to do with the tragic consequences of a love triangle than the missing mortgage of the title, so it probably was not a reworking of the earlier detective story about the hidden necklace. However, the "complicated story" about knights may have inspired the Philippe (Count of Darkness) series. Although Fitzgerald was proud of his knowledge of French history, his writing suffered when he had to rely only on research and his imagination, as the Philippe stories prove.

Fitzgerald's second extant piece of writing, "Reade, Substitute Right Half," was published in *Now and Then* in February 1910. He had discovered that triumph on the playing field and social success were linked. He participated in baseball, football, and basketball and even boxed, but, as one of his contemporaries remembered, he "certainly was no athlete."[33] The *Thoughtbook* confirms Fitzgerald's interest in staying physically fit when, in the section discussing all the clubs he started, he mentions clearing out part of Cecil Read's basement for a gymnasium, which "was quite creditable. It consisted of 4 pairs dumb bells, 2 pairs Indian clubs, 2 pairs (8 gloves) boxing gloves, 1 pair [w]rist exercisers, 1 punching bag, 1 wall exerciser, 1 trapeze, 1 pair swinging rings." Quite creditable indeed—but whatever regime Fitzgerald followed, it did not give him notoriety on the athletic field.

In response to his lack of physical prowess, Fitzgerald philosophized "that if you weren't able to function in action you might at least be able to tell about it, because you felt the same intensity—it was a back door way out of facing reality."[34] In "Reade, Substitute Right Half," the central figure is "a light haired stripling," like Fitzgerald, who manages to come off the bench and score the winning touchdown, unlike Fitzgerald. Perhaps not coincidentally, Cecil Read was one of Fitzgerald's St. Paul friends. Fitzgerald and his buddies played football in Nathan Hale Park, just across the street from the Reads' house on Portland Avenue, where the clubs Fitzgerald organized frequently met. Ironically, Fitzgerald misspells Read's last name several times in the *Thoughtbook* as "Reade."

The next month, in March 1910, Fitzgerald followed with another pastiche similar to the "Mystery of the Raymond Mortgage." Instead of imitating his favorite detective stories, "A Debt of Honor" fell more in line with the G. A. Henty historical fiction books he purchased "by earning twenty-five cents a day from his Aunt Clara McQuillan for eating raw eggs during a vacation in the Catskill Mountains."[35] Having developed a southern bias after listening to his father's somewhat exaggerated tales of the Civil War, Fitzgerald told in "A Debt of Honor" the story of a young southern soldier's heroics at the battle of Chancellorsville.

Because the first seven pages of the *Thoughtbook* are missing, it's hard to say exactly when he began keeping the journal, but most likely it came between "A Debt of Honor" and his fourth and last story published in *Now and Then*, another Civil War-related story called "The Room with the Green Blinds." Since a fifteen-month lag existed between the two Civil War stories, it seems entirely possible that Scott's literary activities during that period were focused on the *Thoughtbook*. And because the *Thoughtbook* contains transcribed portions of an even earlier diary, it serves as an important record of Fitzgerald's development as a writer. Toward the end of his life, he commented on these beginning efforts:

> One's influences are largely literary, but the point where the personal note emerges can come very young (*vide* Keats). I'll go further than that. I believe that with the natural prose writer it might very well come long before twenty, depending upon the amount of awareness with which it is looked for . . . my mother did me the disservice of throwing away all but two of my very young efforts—way back at twelve or thirteen, and later I found that

> the surviving fragments had more quality than some of the stuff written in the tightened-up days of seven or eight years later.[36]

Bouncing between influences "largely literary" in "The Mystery of the Raymond Mortgage," "A Debt of Honor," and "The Room with the Green Blinds" to those where "the personal note emerges," partially in "Reade" and definitely in the *Thoughtbook*, Fitzgerald clearly showed at a young age that his better fiction would develop from the "personal note" rather than any "literary" influences. His worst professional efforts, such as the Philippe series or Civil War stories published late in his career like "A Night at Chancellorsville" or "Thumbs Up," confirm what the earliest examples of his writing indicate: Fitzgerald's talents lay in the interweaving of his own experiences into the warp and woof of his fiction. While "The Mystery of the Raymond Mortgage" "reflects the young author's taste by unintentionally burlesquing the popular nineteenth-century detective story tradition from Edgar Allan Poe to Sir Arthur

Conan Doyle, Maurice Leblanc, Gaston Leroux, and Anna Katherine Green,"[37] it is overly plotted and for the most part absurd. On the other hand, the *Thoughtbook* provides the occasional crystal-ball-like view of the future professional writer. Because the *Thoughtbook* recounts events that occurred at several different points in Fitzgerald's life, we get a glimpse into how he handles temporal shifts. We see his early attempts at creating tension and conflict in the story, as well his choices in wrapping up scenes.[38] The clearest literary connection between the *Thoughtbook* and Fitzgerald's later writings is the way he crafts his dialogue.

In one of the more often quoted pieces of the *Thoughtbook*, Fitzgerald wrote:

> "Violet," I began, "Did you call me a brat."
>
> "No".
>
> "Did you say that you wanted your ring and your picture and your hair back."
>
> "No"
>
> "Did you say that you hated me"

> "Of course not, is that what you went home for".
>
> "No, but Archie Mudge told me those things yesterday evening."
>
> "He's a little scamp" said Violet Indignantly.
>
> At this juncture Elenor Mitchell almost went into hysterics because Jack was teasing her and Violet had to go home with her. That afternoon I spanked Archie Mudge and finished making up with Violet.

The lines are memorable because they sound natural and completely plausible, just the kind of dialogue that fills the pages of Fitzgerald's novels. The scene also shows an extraordinary amount of confidence, both in that the young Scott got the answers he was expecting and that he felt at liberty to punish Archie Mudge for his transgressions.

After his experiment with the *Thoughtbook* and his tangential use of family history in a story about John Wilkes Booth called "The Room with the Green Blinds"[39] in the

June 1911 *Now and Then*, Fitzgerald turned to drama as his creative outlet. Scott had always been fond of playacting. He mentions attending plays in the *Thoughtbook*, presenting a drama based on Arsène Lupin (a popular detective of the day) in the house of his friend Teddy Ames,[40] and producing skits in Cecil Read's attic on Portland Avenue.[41] At the end of the summer of 1911, he wrote the first of four annual plays for St. Paul's Elizabethan Dramatic Club: *The Girl from Lazy J*. Many of the children whose names appear in the *Thoughtbook* took part in these dramas. *The Girl from Lazy J* featured Margaret Armstrong, Dorothy Greene, and Richard Washington. Fitzgerald himself took on the role of Jack Darcy, the nephew of the owner of the eponymous ranch.[42] Elizabeth Magoffin directed the neighborhood children in the living room of her house at 540 Summit Avenue.

That fall, just before his fifteenth birthday, Scott attended Newman Academy. A note in one of his schoolbooks now owned by the Minnesota Historical Society shows a bit of a change in his usual confident style. "Playwrit/poet, Novelist, essayist, philosopher," he penned on the back flyleaf of his copy of George Washington's "Farewell Address" and Daniel Webster's "Bunker Hill Oration," then he continued, "loafer, useless, disagreeable, silly, talented, weak, strong, clever, trivial, a waste, In short a very parody, a mockery of one who might have been more but, whom nature . . . made less . . . with apologies for living, Francis Scott Fitzgerald."

The ending is frightening but clearly reflects the occasional mood of the hero of the Basil Duke Lee stories, who gets his ego bruised a few times. "He Thinks He's Wonderful," for example, is set "in the twelfth year of the century" after Basil "had an unhappy year at school,"[43] exactly the time Fitzgerald was attending Newman. In the story, Fitzgerald introduces Ermine Gilberte Labouisse Bibble, a character drawn from the *Thoughtbook*'s Violet Stockton. Margaret Torrence is based on Marie Hersey. In the story, Basil loses Miss Bibble, just as Fitzgerald does in the *Thoughtbook* when he writes: "Not much has happened since

Violent went away. The day she went away was my birthday and she gave me a box of candy. Her latest fancy is Arther Foley. He has her ring. She wrote him a letter to ask for his picture." "Growing unpopular," he mused in the *Ledger* for July 1912.

The summer of 1912 and his ego were saved by his second play for the Elizabethan Dramatic Club. The curtain rose on *The Captured Shadow* on August 23, 1912, at Mrs. Backus' School for Girls (Oak Hall), where he had attended dances with Margaret Armstrong, according to the *Thoughtbook*. The dialogue, introduction of expository material, and plot in *The Captured Shadow* were handled significantly better than in *The Girl from Lazy J*. A local newspaper even noted "the young author's cleverness" in an article about how the performance had raised $60 for the Baby Welfare Association."[44] In the play, Fitzgerald introduced the gentleman-crook who wins the heart of the heroine, a precursor to such stories as "The Off-Shore Pirate." Once again, the cast included many of the children whose names appear throughout the *Thoughtbook*, including Lawrence Boardman, Margaret Winchester, Dorothy Greene, Paul Ballion, Eleanor Alair, James Porterfield, John Mitchell, George Squires, and Julia Dorr.

His play for 1913 provided even more of incentive for Fitzgerald to see himself as a writer. Speaking at Fitzgerald's reburial next to many of his ancestors at a Rockville, Maryland, cemetery, Scottie noted that her father's "first success as a writer came with the production in St. Paul of a Civil War play, *The Coward*."[45] The play features a reluctant warrior who comes to his senses to protect his southern home from the depredations of the North. The venue had switched to the St. Paul YWCA, where $150 was raised for the Baby Welfare Association on August 29, 1913. A rehearsal picture in a local newspaper called the actors the "children of prominent St. Paul families."[46] A few days later an encore performance was scheduled at the White Bear Lake Yacht Club, where a crowd of three hundred "was even more enthusiastic than that which witnessed the opening performance."[47] As before, Fitzgerald's friends who appear in the *Thoughtbook* made up the cast: Robert Clark, Dorothy Greene, Gustave Schurmeier, Lawrence Boardman, Eleanor Alair, Katherine Schulze, Wharton Smith, and Julia Dorr.

Even after enrolling at Princeton the fall after the production of *The Coward*, Fitzgerald returned to St. Paul the following summer and wrote one more play directed by Elizabeth Magoffin. Performed once again at the YWCA Auditorium and the White Bear Lake Yacht Club, *Assorted Spirits* concerns a costumed man who shows up at the wrong address, foreshadowing "The Camel's Back." Among the cast are *Thoughtbook* regulars Gustave Schurmeier, John Mitchell, Robert Clark, Eleanor Alair, Dorothy Greene, Margaret Armstrong and Betty Mudge.

"A writer wastes nothing," Fitzgerald wrote to Sheilah Graham later in his life.[48] The *Thoughtbook* is a case in point. It provided Fitzgerald with scenes and ideas for his first series, the Basil stories. An episode from "That Kind of Party," an unpublished Basil story for which Fitzgerald changed the names to try to get it published, is reminiscent of Robin's party in the *Thoughtbook*, where Fitzgerald wins the affection of Kiddy Williams:

> "I'm beginning to think you played kissing games," Mr. Tipton guessed casually.
>
> "Oh, they had a crazy game they called Clap-in-and-clap-out," said Terrence indiscreetly.
>
> "What's that?"
>
> "Well, all the boys go out and they say somebody has a letter. No, that's post office. Anyhow, they have to come in and guess who sent for them." Hating himself for the disloyalty to the great experience, he tried to end with: "And then they kneel down and if he's wrong they clap him out of the room. Can I have some more gravy please?"
>
> "But what if he's right?"
>
> "Oh, he's supposed to hug them." Terrence mumbled. It sounded so shameful—it had been so lovely.

In another of the Basil stories, "The Scandal Detectives," Cecil Read, Reuben Warner, and Paul Ballion serve as models for Ripley Buckner, Hubert Blair, and Bill Kampf. The *Thoughtbook*, which Fitzgerald kept locked under his bed, became "The Book of Scandal."

Besides pulling scenes from the *Thoughtbook* for his fiction, Fitzgerald continued to experiment with narrative devices he introduced in it. "The Luckless Santa Clause," which Fitzgerald dated Christmas 1912 and published in *Newman News*, begins: "Miss Harmon was responsible for the whole thing. If it had not been for her foolish whim, Talbot would not have made a fool of himself, and—but I am getting ahead of my story."[49] In the first section of the *Thoughtbook* dated August 1910 and titled "My Girls," Fitzgerald is discussing Kitty Williams when he writes: "Along in a box with them is a lock of hair—but wait I'll come to that." Similarly, in the second section of the *Thoughtbook*, entitled "Indians and Violet" and dated September 1910, Fitzgerald refers to a 1908 summer flirtation with Violet Stockton, who had come from Atlanta to spend the summer with her aunt and uncle, the Finches. In the middle of the story about Violet, Fitzgerald begins to digress about one of his favorite topics: who likes whom best. As he points out that his popularity has begun to wane with several of the girls, he writes, "However I am wandering from the subject."

The fact that Fitzgerald first introduces a femme fatale in a story that that uses the device of pulling back the narrator in much the same way he did in his stories about Kitty and Violet could be coincidental but is nonetheless intriguing. Dorothy Harmon, the femme fatale in "The Luckless Santa Claus," is described in only the vaguest terms, but the narrative implies she is the bored fiancée of the indolent, rich Harry Talbot, who does little more than rack up bills, play golf, and dance. In the tenor of "The Offshore Pirate," Talbot must complete a quest in order to prove to Dorothy he is more than "an empty suit of clothes," to paraphrase a line from "Bernice Bobs Her Hair."

Two other items in the *Thoughtbook* end up in *This Side of Paradise*: locks of hair and rings. During the two years Amory Blaine spends in Minneapolis as "The Young Egotist," Fitzgerald writes, "He collected locks of hair from many girls. He wore the rings of several."[50] Scott has Violet's ring at the beginning of his entries about her in the *Thoughtbook*, but by the end Art Foley does. Later in the *Thoughtbook*, Fitzgerald notes that a lock of Margaret Armstrong's hair is glued to the page.

Another Fitzgerald trademark is introduced in the *Thoughtbook*: lists. Several find their way into the *Thoughtbook*, mostly lists of names. In the *Crack-Up* articles, Fitzgerald explains how important lists were to him:

> It was not an unhappy time. I went away and there were fewer people. I found I was good-and-tired. I could lie around and was glad to, sleeping or dozing sometimes twenty hours a day and in the intervals trying resolutely not to think—instead I made lists—made lists and tore them up, hun-

> dreds of lists: of cavalry leaders and football players and cities, and popular tunes and pitchers, and happy times, and hobbies and houses lived in and how many suits since I left the army and how many pairs of shoes. . . . And lists of women I'd liked, and of times I had let myself be snubbed by people who had not been my betters in character or ability.
>
> —And then suddenly, surprisingly, I got better.[51]

One of his most famous lists occurs near the end of *The Great Gatsby*, when he lists the party invitations students exchange at Union Station in Chicago. "Are you going to the Ordways'? the Herseys'? the Schultzes'?" the eager travelers ask. All three families have deep St. Paul roots. The latter two are central to the *Thoughtbook*, and, ironically, as in the *Thoughtbook*, Fitzgerald misspells the Schulzes' name.

Notes

1 Matthew J. Bruccoli, *Some Sort of Epic Grandeur: The Life of F. Scott Fitzgerald* (New York: Harcourt Brace Jovanovich, 1981), 357.

2 Andrew Turnbull, ed., *The Letters of F. Scott Fitzgerald* (New York: Charles Scribner's Sons, 1965), 503.

3 Malcolm Cowley, "Fitzgerald: The Romance of Money," in *A Second Flowering: Works and Days of the Lost Generation* (New York: Viking, 1973), 78. Fitzgerald's *Ledger* covers the same event in much the same way in an entry in March 1908. Although Fitzgerald claimed in his *Ledger* that he gave his swimming money back to his mother after hearing his father tell his mother over the phone that he had lost his job, by June of the that year he was playing "golf with Inky on the public links." F. Scott Fitzgerald, *F. Scott Fitzgerald's Ledger: A Facsimile* (Washington, D.C.: A Bruccoli Clark book, 1973), 162. "Inky" was James Imham, a friend mentioned in the *Thoughtbook*.

4 Cowley, 86.

5 "Summit Av.," *Minneapolis Star Tribune*, July 9, 1995, 26A.

6 Bryant Mangum, *A Fortune Yet: Money in the Art of F. Scott Fitzgerald's Short Stories* (New York: Garland Publishing, Inc., 1991), 10.

7 F. Scott Fitzgerald, *The Great Gatsby* (New York: Scribner, 2004 [1925]), 35.

8 Ibid., 57.

9 F. Scott Fitzgerald, *The Crack-Up* (New York: New Directions, 1945), 69.

10 Cowley, 87.

11 Ron Rosenbaum, "A Wilderness of Errol," *Smithsonian* (March 2012): 13.

12 John Kuehl, "Scott Fitzgerald's Critical Opinions," *Modern Fiction Studies* (Spring 1961): 14.

13 Mangum, 12.

14 Ibid.

15 Ibid., 20.

16 F. Scott Fitzgerald, *This Side of Paradise* (New York: Charles Scribner's Sons, 1948 [1920]), 54.

17 Ibid., 50.

18 Fitzgerald, *The Great Gatsby*, 6.

19 Mangum, 47.

20 "Marriage of Miss McQuillan to Mr. Edward Fitzgerald," *Washington Post*, February 13, 1890, 5. Property records seem to indicate this property was not owned by the McQuillans. The address is now occupied by a newer apartment building.

21 An undated newspaper clipping in the McQuillan file located at the Minnesota History Center states: "The pavement of the walks leading to this home at Tenth and John Streets was composed of shells. A curious crowd was found in early times near the house on Sundays and the holidays inspecting the peculiar construction. The structure, which is now Luther hospital, was the home of P.J. [*sic*] McQuillan, a pioneer grocery dealer of St. Paul."

22 "The company had no advertisement in the directory, which is surprising, since almost every business in town advertised there. I spot-checked the papers for ads but could not find any. I also looked through local furniture catalogs of the time and found no mention of it. There was no information on Henze, Otis, or Denegre [the vice presidents and treasurer listed in the City Directory]

in our biography or obituary files." Carolyn Gilman, letter to Scottie Fitzgerald Smith, September 5, 1976, located at Minnesota History Center.

23 *Celebrating the Cairo: 1894–1994* (Washington, D.C.: Coleman Design Group, n.d.), 8. In June 1917, Scott met his cousin Ceci at the Cairo. He sent her several poems from Princeton University on June 10, 1917, and at the end he wrote, "One more thing—the most sincere apologies for the cold you got listening to my inane ramblings (of course I didn't *really* think they were inane) on the porch of the Cairo." Turnbull, ed., *The Letters of F. Scott Fitzgerald,* 415.

24 Matthew Bruccoli, ed., *A Life in Letters* (New York: Scribner, 1995), 5.

25 Bruccoli, *Some Sort of Epic Grandeur,* 22.

26 See Dave Page and Jack Koblas, *Toward the Summit: F. Scott Fitzgerald in Minnesota* (St. Cloud, Minn.: North Star Press, 1996).

27 Bruccoli, *Some Sort of Epic Grandeur,* 30.

28 The "shriveled spinster" in the short story "The Spire and the Gargoyle" who asks the narrator to which college she should send her nephew was inspired by Annabel McQuillan. John Kuehl, *The Apprentice Fiction of F. Scott Fitzgerald* (New Brunswick, N.J.: Rutgers University Press, 1965), 111.

29 Bruccoli, *Some Sort of Epic Grandeur,* 37.

30 Benjamin Griggs, interview with Jack Koblas, April 10, 1976.

31 Bob Clark, letter to Jack Koblas, May 17, 1976.

32 Norris Jackson, interview with the author, August 16, 1982.

33 Jean Ingersoll Summersby, letter to Jack Koblas, November 12, 1976.

34 Kuehl, *The Apprentice Fiction of F. Scott Fitzgerald,* 29.

35 Bruccoli, *Some Sort of Epic Grandeur,* 19. Armory in *This Side of Para-*

dise "had all the Henty biases in history" (17), meaning that he was for the Southern Confederacy" (25).

36 Henry Dan Piper, *F. Scott Fitzgerald: A Critical Portrait* (New York: Holt, Rinehart, and Winston, 1963), 29. The "fragments" to which Fitzgerald refers, according to Piper, are from the *Thoughtbook*.

37 Kuehl, *The Apprentice Fiction of F. Scott Fitzgerald*, 18.

38 For a discussion of the literary qualities of the *Thoughtbook*, see John R. Kuehl, "Scott Fitzgerald's 'Thoughtbook,'" *Thoughtbook of F. Scott Fitzgerald* (Princeton, N.J.: Princeton University Library, 1965).

39 Edward Fitzgerald's cousin had married John Surratt, the son of Mary Surratt, who was hanged for complicity in Lincoln's murder. Dr. Samuel Mudd had introduced John Wilkes Booth to John Surratt, since the latter was a Confederate courier and Booth wanted to play his greatest role in the country's deadliest drama. Once Fitzgerald had gained prominence as a writer, "his parents wanted him to write a book exonerating Mrs. Suratt, but he said she was either guilty or a fool and in neither case was he interested." Turnbull, ed., *The Letters of F. Scott Fitzgerald*, 6.

40 Fitzgerald immortalized the Ames house in his short story "The Scandal Detectives."

41 Alan Margolies, *F. Scott Fitzgerald's St. Paul Plays, 1911–1914* (Princeton, N.J.: Princeton University Library, 1978), 5.

42 During the last year of his life, Fitzgerald wrote Arnold Gingrich at *Esquire* to ask if he thought it might be good to use a pseudonym—"say John Darcy." In *F. Scott Fitzgerald's St. Paul Plays*, Margolies speculates that Scott might have been thinking of this early play at the time (13).

43 F. Scott Fitzgerald, "He Thinks He's Wonderful," *The Basil and Josephine Stories* (New York: Charles Scribner's Sons, 1973), 77.

44 "Play Helps Babies," *St. Paul Pioneer Press*, August 24, 1912, 9.

45 Scottie Fitzgerald Smith, "The Colonial Ancestors of Francis Scott Key Fitzgerald," *Maryland Historical Magazine* (Winter 1981): 374.

46 Matthew J. Bruccoli et al., eds. *The Romantic Egoists: A Pictorial Autobiography from the Scrapbooks and Albums of Scott and Zelda Fitzgerald* (New York: Charles Scribner's Sons, 1974), 18.

47 Ibid., 19.

48 Larry W. Phillips, ed., *F. Scott Fitzgerald on Writing* (New York: Charles Scribner's Sons, 1985), 28.

49 Kuehl, *The Apprentice Fiction of F. Scott Fitzgerald*, 48.

50 Fitzgerald, *This Side of Paradise*, 17.

51 Fitzgerald, *The Crack-Up*, 71–72.

F. Scott Fitzgerald was born in 1896 at 481 Laurel Avenue in St. Paul's Ramsey Hill neighborhood. He attended St. Paul Academy and chronicled his adventures and romantic interests in a secret journal he called the *Thoughtbook*, which was kept locked in a box beneath his bed; the *Thoughtbook* was later the basis for "The Book of Scandal" in his Basil Duke Lee stories. His first published novel, *This Side of Paradise*, revised while he lived on Summit Avenue, also depicts scenes reminiscent of his adolescence in the Twin Cities. Often praised as one of the greatest writers of the twentieth century, he is best known for his 1925 novel *The Great Gatsby*, which epitomizes the Jazz Age; he also wrote *The Beautiful and the Damned*, *Tender Is the Night*, *The Last Tycoon*, and many short story collections. He died in 1940.

Dave Page is coauthor, with John J. Koblas, of *F. Scott Fitzgerald in Minnesota: Toward the Summit* and coeditor, with Patricia Hampl, of *The St. Paul Stories of F. Scott Fitzgerald*. He teaches writing and lectures on Fitzgerald at national and international venues.

The Thoughtbook of F. Scott Fitzgerald was designed and set in type by Chris Long at Mighty Media, Minneapolis. The typefaces used are from the Vendetta type family, designed by John Downer for Emigre, Inc.